Rookie choices™

THE COOL COATS

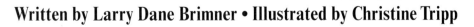

The Corner Kids

Written by Larry Dane Brimner • Illustrated by Christine Tripp

Children's Press®
A Division of Scholastic Inc.
New York • Toronto • London • Auckland • Sydney
Mexico City • New Delhi • Hong Kong
Danbury, Connecticut

For the cool kids at Ivey Ranch School
—L.D.B.

For my uncle, Leonard White
—C.T.

Reading Consultants
Linda Cornwell
Literacy Specialist

Katharine A. Kane
Education Consultant
(Retired, San Diego County Office of Education and San Diego State University)

Library of Congress Cataloging-in-Publication Data

Brimner, Larry Dane.
  The cool coats / written by Larry Dane Brimner ; illustrated by Christine Tripp.
      p. cm.
Summary: Jealous of his friends's matching coats, Alex soon realizes
how fortunate he is to have a warm coat when so many people have none.
  ISBN 0-516-22545-6 (lib. bdg.)   0-516-27834-7 (pbk.)
  [1. Coats—Fiction. 2. Gratitude—Fiction.] I. Tripp, Christine, ill. II. Title.
  PZ7.B767 Cj 2003
  [E]—dc21
                              2002008260

CHILDREN'S PRESS, AND ROOKIE CHOICES™, and associated logos are trademarks
and or registered trademarks of Grolier Publishing Co., Inc. SCHOLASTIC and associated
logos are trademarks and or registered trademarks of Scholastic Inc.
1 2 3 4 5 6 7 8 9 10 R 12 11 10 09 08 07 06 05 04 03

This book is about **thankfulness.**

Alex and Gabby waited in the apartment lobby for Three J. The three friends walked to school together every morning.

When the elevator doors opened, Alex looked at Three J. He blinked his eyes. He looked at Gabby. "I'm seeing double," he said.

Gabby and Three J looked at each other then, too. They had on matching coats.

"Cool coat," Gabby and Three J said to each other. Then they laughed like it was the best joke ever.

9

Alex thought about his own coat. It wasn't blue. It didn't have a furry hood.

All of a sudden he didn't feel like one of the Corner Kids. That's what the three friends called themselves because they lived on corners of the same street.

Alex thought about the blue
coats all the way to school.
They *were* cool.

He thought about the coats
all day long. If he had a coat
like theirs, all three Corner Kids
could look alike.

"Mom!" Alex shouted when he got home from school.

His mom peeked out from her office.

"I need a new coat," Alex said.

"That is a new coat," she said. "It's the one you wanted."

"I know," said Alex. "But now I need one like Gabby's and Three J's."

19

"I'm sorry, Alex," she said. "But we can't afford to buy another coat."

Alex sighed. He stomped to his room.

Alex was still in a bad mood the next morning.

After breakfast, he got ready
for school.

"You know," his mom said softly,
"not everyone is lucky enough
to have a new, warm coat."

Alex thought about that. It was true. He had seen pictures on TV of people who didn't have much at all.

He looked around at his own nice room. He snugged his coat tighter around himself. He *was* lucky.

"I'm sorry," he said quietly. Then he hugged his mom.

27

Later, Three J asked if Alex wanted to trade coats for the day.

Alex shook his head. He knew his own coat was cool, too.

ABOUT THE AUTHOR

Larry Dane Brimner studied literature and writing at San Diego State University and taught school for twenty years. The author of more than seventy-five books for children, many of them Children's Press titles, he enjoys meeting young readers and writers when he isn't at his computer.

ABOUT THE ILLUSTRATOR

Christine Tripp lives in Ottawa, Canada, with her husband Don; four grown children—Elizabeth, Erin, Emily, and Eric; son-in-law Jason; grandsons Brandon and Kobe; four cats; and one very large, scruffy puppy named Jake.